Echoes of the Past

How Evolution Shaped Your Mind

Freudian Trips

Copyright Page

© 2023 by Freudian Trips

All rights reserved. No part of this book may be reproduced in any form or by any electronic or mechanical means, including information storage and retrieval systems, without permission in writing from the publisher, except by a reviewer who may quote brief passages in a review.

This book is a work of non-fiction. Unless otherwise noted, the author and the publisher make no explicit guarantees as to the accuracy of the information contained in this book and will not be held responsible for any errors or omissions.

Published by Omniterra Media Inc

First Edition

Visit the author's website at www.freudiantrips.com

Disclaimer

The views and opinions expressed in this book are those of the author(s) and do not necessarily reflect the official policy or position of any other agency, organization, employer, or company. The contents of this book are for informational and educational purposes only and are not intended to serve as professional advice, diagnosis, or treatment.

The information provided in this book is believed to be accurate and reliable as of the date of publication. However, it may include some errors or inaccuracies, and no warranty or guarantee is provided regarding the accuracy, timeliness, or applicability of the content.

Readers are encouraged to consult with professional philosophers, educators, or other qualified professionals where appropriate for personalized advice. The author(s) and publisher shall not be liable for any loss, damage, or harm caused or alleged to be caused, directly or indirectly, by the information or ideas contained, suggested, or referenced in this book.

By reading this book, the reader acknowledges and agrees that they are solely responsible for how they interpret and apply the information contained herein.

This book may also include references to other works, studies, and sources. These references are provided for further reading and exploration and do not imply endorsement or validation of the specific theories, viewpoints, or interpretations presented in those works.

Introduction: Unlocking the Secrets of the Evolved Mind

Imagine you could travel back in time. Not just a few decades or centuries, but thousands and thousands of years. You find yourself in a world where our human ancestors roamed – hunting, gathering, and striving to survive amidst challenges we can barely fathom. This was the world that shaped our minds.

Darwin's Discovery: The Engine of Change

In the 1800s, a scientist named Charles Darwin unlocked a powerful secret about life: evolution by natural selection. It's a simple idea with huge implications. Imagine animals with slightly different traits – some run faster, some have sharper teeth. Those best suited to their environment are more likely to survive, have offspring, and pass on their successful traits. Over time, generation after generation, this process shapes entire species.

Darwin changed how we see the natural world, but what about our psychology - our thoughts, feelings, and behaviors?

Evolutionary Psychology: Our Minds on a Journey

This is where evolutionary psychology comes in. It's like a detective story, but instead of solving crimes, we're solving the mysteries of the human mind. Evolutionary psychologists believe that our brains, just like our bodies, have been sculpted by the challenges of survival and reproduction over countless generations.

Those ancestors whose minds helped them find food, attract mates, and stay safe were more likely to have children and pass on their mental 'toolkit'. Bit by bit, over vast stretches of time, these inherited brain tools shaped who we are today.

The Power of Adaptation: More Than Meets the Eye

Adaptation is about more than just having big muscles or sharp claws. Think of the butterflies that blend into tree bark to hide from predators. Our minds have adaptations too! They come in the form of instincts, emotions, and ways of thinking that helped our ancestors meet the challenges of their time.

The Ancient World Within Us

The key concept here is the Environment of Evolutionary Adaptedness (EEA). This is the world our minds were designed for – the challenges and conditions faced by those early humans. It's a world very different from the modern one, full of dangers and opportunities that modern people rarely encounter. Yet, the mental tools we inherited from those times still influence how we think and act today!

The Adventure Begins

This book is an invitation to explore that ancient world within you. We'll uncover the hidden instincts that drive our decisions, the emotions that protect us, and the deep social wiring that connects us. You'll see why we think, feel, and do the things we do in a whole new light.

Ready to begin? Let's dive into how evolution has shaped the fascinating landscape of the human mind!

Chapter 1: The Mind's Blueprint – How Evolution Built Our Brains

Think of your brain as an incredibly complex survival machine. It's filled with programs, circuits, and automatic responses, all fine-tuned over countless generations. This chapter is about how those programs got there and why they are fundamental to understanding ourselves.

Natural Selection: The Mind's Architect

Remember Darwin's idea of natural selection? It's not just about bodies! Our brains were shaped by the same forces. Imagine our ancestors facing life-or-death challenges: finding food, avoiding predators, making friends, and finding mates. Those with the mental edge, even a slight one, were more likely to survive and pass on their genes.

Over immense stretches of time, this process sculpted our minds, favoring thoughts, feelings, and actions that promoted our ancestors' survival and reproduction. It's like nature constantly upgraded our mental software!

Psychological Adaptations: Tools for Living

Just like animals have physical adaptations – camouflage, speed, venom – humans have psychological adaptations. These are mental mechanisms that evolved to solve specific problems faced by our ancestors. Let's look at some examples:

- **Fear of Snakes:** Many people are instinctively afraid of snakes, even if they've never been harmed by one. This fear was likely adaptive in the past when venomous snakes were a real threat.
- **Sweet Tooth:** Our love of sweet foods motivated ancestors to seek out ripe fruits, rich in energy. While now this instinct can lead to overeating, it was valuable in times of scarcity.

Universal Human Nature: What We All Share

While we're all unique, there's a bedrock of shared human psychology. These are fundamental mental modules present in all humans across cultures. They include things like:

- **Language:** We're born ready to learn language, a complex skill crucial for survival and cooperation.
- **Cooperation:** We have a strong instinct to work with others toward shared goals, making us far more effective than lone wolves.
- **Emotions:** The basic emotions of fear, anger, joy, and sadness are universal – they guide our actions and communicate with others.

Instincts and Drives: Listen to Your Inner Voice

Instincts are like pre-programmed urges driving our behavior. Here are some examples:

- **Hunger and Thirst:** Powerful physical drives for survival.
- **Sex Drive:** Ensures reproduction and the passing on of genes.
- **Protectiveness of Kin:** Intense drive to protect children and family.

The Mating Game: Men, Women, and Evolution

Men and women have faced slightly different evolutionary challenges, especially when it comes to reproduction. This led to some fundamental differences in our evolved mating psychology:

- **Parental Investment:** Women invest far more biologically in having children (pregnancy, breastfeeding). This makes them generally pickier when choosing a mate, seeking resources and stability.
- **Short-term vs. Long-term Strategies:** Due to less biological investment, men evolved to be more open to short-term mating, but they also seek partners who can have healthy children.

These factors shape our attraction, what we look for in partners, and sometimes lead to conflict and misunderstandings.

It's Only the Beginning

This chapter gave you a quick blueprint of how evolution has shaped our minds. With this foundation, we're ready to explore a fascinating world of hidden instincts, emotions, and social behaviors. Understanding our evolutionary roots will help you decode your own, and others', behavior in a whole new light.

Chapter 2: Decoding Your Feelings: The Evolutionary Power of Emotions

Imagine a life without emotions - no fear to alert you to danger, no joy to reward success, no love to bind us together. Emotions aren't just fleeting experiences; they are ancient guides, shaped by evolution to help us navigate the world.

The Adaptive Value of Emotions: Your Inner Compass

Think of emotions as quick-action programs designed for survival and success. They motivate us, focus our attention, and help us make rapid decisions in complex situations. Here's how some key emotions were our ancestors' secret weapons:

- **Fear:** A jolt of fear triggers a cascade of physical changes. Your heart races, senses sharpen, and you're ready to flee or fight. This helped our ancestors avoid danger and survive threats.
- **Anger:** A surge of anger can make you feel powerful and intimidating. It likely evolved to defend yourself, deter rivals, and protect resources.

- **Jealousy:** This unpleasant emotion can motivate you to guard your mate and valuable relationships, ensuring your reproductive success.
- **Love:** Feelings of deep attachment drive bonding with mates, children, and close allies. Love promotes the kind of cooperation and protection that were critical for survival.

Emotions: The Steering Wheel of Decisions

We like to think we make decisions with pure logic, but emotions often hold the wheel! Think about it – your gut feelings often guide you before you weigh all the facts. This is because our ancestors didn't have the luxury of endless analysis. Rapid emotional responses, sometimes followed by careful thinking, gave them an edge.

Even today, emotions shape our choices - from what we eat to the risks we take, to who we trust and who we decide to befriend.

The Language of the Face: Universal Emotions

While our cultures may differ wildly, there's a universal language of emotions that transcends borders. Researchers have found that people all around the world – even in isolated tribes – recognize and express core emotions like joy, sadness, fear, and anger in remarkably similar ways.

Why? Because the ability to signal your feelings honestly was vital for forming alliances and navigating the complexities of social life within a group.

Mind Readers: Decoding the Emotions of Others

Just as we express emotions, we're amazingly good at reading them in others. We pick up on subtle facial expressions, body language, and tone of voice. This "mind-reading" ability is another evolutionary gift. It allowed our ancestors to quickly assess threats, gauge the mood of the tribe, and cooperate effectively.

The Emotional Rollercoaster: When Feelings Go Off Track

While emotions were vital for our ancestors, they can sometimes get us into trouble in the modern world. Imagine extreme road rage (anger), debilitating phobias (fear), or destructive jealousy. These are examples of ancient emotional programs misfiring in an environment drastically different from the one we evolved for.

Exploring Your Emotional Landscape

This chapter is just the start of understanding your emotions from an evolutionary perspective. With this knowledge, you can gain valuable insight into your motivations, how you react in different situations, and even how to recognize and navigate the emotional world of others.

Chapter 3: The Social Animal: Cooperation, Competition, and the Dance of Human Interaction

Think about your friendships, rivalries, social groups, and the way you act around strangers. It might feel far removed from evolution, but the way we interact with others is deeply rooted in our ancient past. This chapter reveals the hidden forces shaping our social world.

Cooperation & Altruism: Beyond Selfishness

We often see evolution as "survival of the fittest", picturing a cutthroat struggle. But humans have a remarkable capacity for cooperation and altruism – helping others, even at a cost to ourselves. Why would evolution favor this? Here's where it gets exciting:

- **Reciprocity: "I'll Scratch Your Back..."** If you help someone, they're more likely to help you in the future. This "you scratch my back, I'll scratch yours" system benefited our ancestors who relied on each other for survival.

- **Kin Selection: Family First** Humans are incredibly protective of their family. This makes sense – your relatives share your genes! Helping them ensures some of your own genetic code is passed on, even if you don't have children yourself.

Competition & Status: Climbing the Ladder

While cooperation is vital, humans also have a competitive streak. Think of striving for top grades, the dream job, or respect in your community. This drive for status likely has evolutionary roots too. Our ancestors who gained resources, mates, and influence were more likely to survive and reproduce. This explains why we still care so much about where we stand in the social pecking order.

- **Dominance Hierarchies: Who's in Charge** Many social groups, from ancient tribes to modern workplaces, form hierarchies. This provides order and reduces conflict. Those at the top have better access to resources key for survival and reproduction.

In-Group vs. Out-Group: Us vs. Them

Sadly, our remarkable ability to cooperate within groups has a dark side – prejudice against outsiders. In our ancestral past, unfamiliar tribes could pose threats to resources or territory. This shaped an instinct to favor our own 'in-group' and be wary of the 'out-group'. While extremely harmful in the modern world, this tribal tendency is wired into our brains.

Strategies for Conflict Resolution: Seeking Harmony

With competition and tribalism built into us, how can we achieve peace? Evolution might have solutions here too:

- **Empathy and Understanding:** The ability to put ourselves in another's shoes and see their perspective fosters cooperation and reduces hostility.
- **Negotiation and Compromise:** Finding mutually beneficial solutions – giving a little, getting a little – likely helped our ancestors navigate social life.
- **Reputation Management:** Humans care deeply about how others perceive them. This means acting fairly and honestly to maintain a good reputation, which has benefits for forming alliances.

Social Navigation in the Modern World

Understanding the evolutionary roots of our social behavior doesn't mean we're trapped by them. With awareness, we can consciously choose to overcome our ancient instincts. We can foster empathy across group boundaries, promote fairness, and work towards a more cooperative world.

Chapter 4: From Ancient Minds to Modern Problems: The Power of Evolutionary Insights

We've traveled through time, explored the mind's inner workings, and uncovered how our social world is shaped by evolution. But what does this mean for your life today? This chapter sheds light on how evolutionary psychology offers solutions to modern-day challenges.

Understanding Mental Disorders: Finding the Roots

Some mental health struggles, like depression, anxiety, or phobias, can feel baffling. But an evolutionary perspective can bring clarity:

- **Mismatched Minds:** Our brains evolved for a very different world. This disconnect between our ancestral past and the demands of modern life can create psychological distress. Imagine an intense fear response that was helpful against jungle predators, but now gets triggered by crowds.
- **Exaggerated Adaptations:** Some mental patterns may be evolved adaptations taken to the extreme.

Mild jealousy is protective, but overwhelming jealousy becomes destructive. This perspective aids in understanding why disorders exist in the first place.

Evolutionary psychology doesn't suggest mental illness is inevitable, but it offers clues for developing more targeted treatments and understanding the root causes.

Relationship Dynamics: Decoding Love & Conflict

Ever wondered why you're drawn to certain people or why some relationships thrive while others fail? Let's look to evolution for answers:

- **What We Find Attractive:** We didn't evolve to like just anyone! We instinctively seek qualities signaling health, good genes, and the ability to be a good parent. While influenced by culture, a lot of what sparks attraction is rooted in evolutionary biology.
- **Conflict & Resolution:** Arguments with partners or friends? Evolutionary psychology can help you understand the clash of mating strategies, mismatched motivations, or different perspectives based on ancestral roles. This awareness can pave the way to better negotiation and healthier relationships.

Consumer World: Why We Buy

Companies spend billions trying to influence your shopping habits. But they're often tapping into ancient instincts you don't even realize you have! Here's how:

- **Status Signals:** Shiny sports cars or designer bags aren't just about the product, they signal the owner's success and resources – making them attractive to potential mates in an evolutionary sense.
- **The Illusion of Scarcity:** "Limited Time Offer" tactics play on our ancestral fear of missing out on valuable resources.
- **Social Proof:** We're heavily influenced by what others do and think. Testimonials and endorsements trigger our instinct to follow the herd, as this was generally safe in the past.

Decoding Persuasion: Arm Yourself With Knowledge

Understanding the evolutionary buttons that advertisers and salespeople try to push gives you power. You'll recognize manipulative tactics and make more conscious decisions based on what you truly need, not what your evolved instincts urge you towards.

Evolutionary Psychology in Action

This chapter only scratches the surface of how our evolved minds impact our modern lives. Evolutionary insights can help us understand ourselves, create healthier relationships, and navigate the world with greater self-awareness. The best part? It doesn't require being a scientist – just a curious mind and the understanding that your everyday behaviors have a fascinating backstory!

Conclusion: The Evolutionary Journey Continues – Challenges and Possibilities

Throughout this book, we've embarked on an extraordinary journey, uncovering the evolutionary roots of our thoughts, feelings, and behaviors. It's a perspective that offers powerful insights, but like any scientific field, evolutionary psychology has its limitations, sparks debate, and faces exciting possibilities for the future.

Limits and Controversies: A Critical Eye

- **The Speculation Factor:** While evolutionary psychology offers compelling explanations, we can't directly test how our minds worked thousands of years ago. Some theories rely on indirect evidence and logical deduction, prompting criticism.
- **Deterministic Thinking:** Some fear that evolutionary psychology implies our behavior is rigidly determined by our genes. However, it acknowledges that environment, culture, and individual choices interact with our evolved predispositions.

- **Sensitive Topics:** When exploring topics like sex differences or tribalism, evolutionary explanations can be misconstrued as justifying harmful behaviors or inequality. It's crucial to emphasize that understanding the origin of a bias doesn't make it acceptable.

The Nature vs. Nurture Dance: Finding Balance

Evolutionary psychology doesn't discount the importance of nurture — our experiences, learning, and culture shape us profoundly. It sees nature and nurture not as opposing forces, but engaged in an intricate dance. Our genes provide a blueprint, but the environment fills in the details. Understanding this interplay is key to a complete picture of the human mind.

The Future of the Field: Exciting Horizons

Evolutionary psychology is still relatively young, with exciting research avenues and applications on the horizon:

- **Neuroscience Partnership:** Combining brain imaging techniques with evolutionary theory reveals how our evolved mental modules manifest in the physical structures of our brains.
- **Solving Modern Problems:** Insights into evolved preferences for cooperation, conflict resolution, and group dynamics could help build more peaceful and inclusive societies.
- **Personalized Medicine:** Understanding how our evolved brains respond differently to environments

could lead to better, more tailored treatments for mental health issues.

Embracing the Evolutionary Perspective: Knowledge is Power

While evolutionary psychology has limitations and must be applied with care, it offers a profound new lens through which to view ourselves and the world around us. By recognizing the ancient instincts whispering within us, we gain the power to make more conscious choices, build stronger relationships, and perhaps create a society where our evolved tendencies work for us, not against us.

The journey of understanding our evolved minds has no end. New discoveries and debates will continue to shape this fascinating field. The most important takeaway? Keep asking questions, think critically, and let the evolutionary perspective deepen your understanding of what makes us human.

About Freudian Trips

Welcome to Freudian Trips, your dedicated platform for diving deep into the world of psychology. We are more than just a YouTube channel or a book publisher. We are a beacon of enlightenment, making complex psychological concepts accessible and engaging for all.

Our YouTube channel is a rich repository of psychology made simple. We take the profound and often complex ideas from the world of psychology and break them down into digestible, easy-to-understand content. From the foundational theories of Freud to the cognitive insights of Piaget, we cover a broad spectrum of psychological schools and thoughts, making psychology accessible to everyone, regardless of their background or prior knowledge.

As a book publisher, we take the same approach, transforming intricate psychological theories into comprehensible narratives. Our books are not just collections of words, but vessels of wisdom that make psychology approachable and relatable. We believe that psychology should not be confined to academic circles, but should be available to all who seek to understand the human mind and behavior.

At Freudian Trips, we believe in the power of curiosity and the pursuit of knowledge. We are here to stoke the fires of your curiosity, to guide you on your intellectual journey, and to help you navigate the fascinating world of psychology.

If you are someone who is not afraid to question, to explore, and to learn, then you are in the right place. Join us on this journey of exploration, as we make psychology easy to understand, one concept at a time.

Be sure to visit our Youtube channel at:
www.freudiantrips.com/youtube

You can also visit us on the web at www.freudiantrips.com

Welcome to The Freudian Trip community. Stay curious. Stay enlightened.